PISA
THROUGH THE CENTURIES

editions ITALCARDS   LA TORRE
bologna - italy   Sole distributor for Pisa

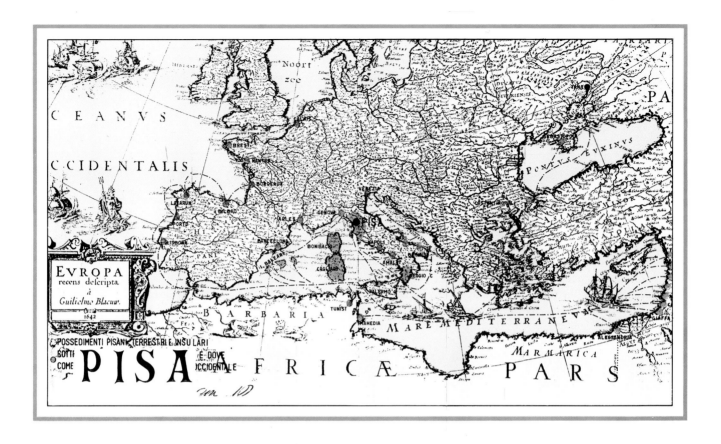

PISA - IST HISTORY

Pisa is divided in two parts by the Arno River. It is at 4 mts above sea-level and located on a fertile plain that extends from the foot of «Monte Pisano» to the sea-coast: which is not more than 8-12 Kms from the town-center. With a population just over one hundrd thousend inhabitants Pisa has a military and civil airport, is an archiepiscopal seat and also boasts a university centre of ancient historical and cultural traditions. The university of Pisa was founded, in fact, in the twelfth century and is, therefore, one of the oldest, and also one of the most glorious, Italian universities. Of a remarkable agricultural and also industrial importance Pisa communicates excellenty with the rest of the peninsula. It is, in fact, a main station on the Rome-Genoa railway line with branches to Empoli-Florence and Siena, as well as on another line, to Lucca-Montecatini Terme-Florence. It is a junction of main and tollroads. That is the reason why from the town the noumerous resorts on the Tyrrhenian Sea and in the mountains are easily accessible. Also the centres for thermal cures are included within an easy reach: S. Giuliano Terme at only 4 Kms, Montecatini and Monsummano Terme at not more than 38-45 Kms.

Regarding the climate that of Pisa can be classified with the most temperate zones of Italy, because the «Monte Pisano», the mountains of «Garfagnana» and the Maritime Alps shelter it from the cold north winds, while the nearby seafront allows it to breathe the temperate west and south winds. As such the town is suitable for a pleasant stay, backed up by a first rate hotel organization and by the opportunity of having within a short range the many spots above mentioned besides other such as Lucca, Torre del Lago Puccini (country-house of the great composer),

Collodi with the monument of Pinocchio and its historical garden, Leghorn, etc., for rich experiences and pleasure trips.

But the town is principally glorified for its ancient and noble past; it is said that Pisa is older than Rome and that it was one of the most powerful marine Republics.

Opinions about its origin are discordant, but one of the more reliable sources gives us to think, that most likely it rose between the 5th and the 7th century B.C. At first it was a Greek colony founded by Phoceans, after an Etruscan one. From 180 B.C. it became a Roman colony and Augustus named it «Colonia Julia Pisana». The fortune of the town was always governed by the sea, that in this period was at the gates of Pisa. From the 11th century Pisa became a powerful marine Republic. That is to say after the period where it was allied with the Romans up to the second Punic war and afterwards when Caesar Octavian established the harbour in a natural bay (the «Sinus Pisanus») and precisely at the estuary of the Arno River where big ships could dock. Up to that time, it had been under Odoacer, the Ostrogothics, the Byzantines, the Longobards and the Franks, then annexed in the Marquisate of Tuscany under the Carolingians.

As a powerful marine Republic, Pisa fought against the Saracens an conquered Corsica, Sardinia and the Balearic Islands; it asserted its high prestige also in the East especially after having partecipated on the 1st Crusade. The problem now was to consolidate and to maintain its influence over the conquered territories and in this intention long and fierce struggles against Amalfi and Genoa for supremacy over lands and sea were never lacking. Added to this constant military effort there was strong internal unrests mainly caused by the Guelf-Tuscan league on account of speculations, of contrast on how the enormous amassed wealth was to be administrated. The result was, that even though they managed resist the Guelf-Free cities and the followers of Guelf, amongst the citizens of Pisa, the town became slowly weaker, so much so that beeing engaged contemporaneously, on the seas of Levant, in rivarly with the Republic of Venice, and on the Mediterranean against Genoa, it suffered a disastrous defeast by Genoa in the famous battle of Meloria in 1284. It was the «day of Saint Sistus» anniversary of many victories, but this time Pisa had lost. The Republic went on, but the glory, prestige and rule of the sea came to an end. In this manner, after an extraordinary adventure, the economical and political decline of Pisa started; broke down the`free-city institutes and in their place the families of nobles asserted their authority: first came the Uguccione della Faggiola, then the Della Gherardesca and after the family Gambacorti. Finally the family D'Appiano ruled over the fortune of Pisa untill it passed over to Visconti, the later ceded it to the authority of Florence in the year 1405.

Although Pisa had now lost its political indipendence, nevertheless, under the wise rule of Medici, the town developped progressively as a cultural and intellettual centre. Cosimo the 1st de' Medici, for instance, renewed the study of the Sapienza. Leopoldo the 2nd reorganized the Scuola Normale Superiore founded by Napoleon in the year 1810.

After so many historical vicissitudes, in the year 1860, Pisa joined the Kingdom of Italy with a solemn plebiscite.

During the 2nd World War the town was subjected to notable destruction from heavy bombing raids and because of the dogged resistance of the Germans on the apposite banks of the Arno River, just within the limits of townwalls. This resistance lasted 40 days. Casualties were very high and the destruction was not limited only to public property but also to artistic treasures. In the field of art the grand «Camposanto Monumentale» (Monumental churchyard), the marble walls of which close off one side of the imposing »Piazza dei Miracoli», was seriously damaged.

A fresco by Aretino Spinello with a detail of S. Efisio's battle against the infidels. On the left one can see S. Efisio's conversion where he is on his knees praying in front of the winged knight (Monumental Cemetery).

PISA: ITS ART I GRANDI PISANI

OF THE TOWN, TOGETHER WITH ITS

In the field of architecture and in that of sculpture Pisa originated the so called «Pisa Style», or also named «Lucca-Pisa Style». The art so highly conceived and expressed opened its great chapter with the architect Buschetto in the 11th century. Then came RAINALDO, in the 12th century, to carry on the work begun by the first, who started the façade of the Cathedral. DIOTISLAVI (heir of the art of Buschetto — initiator of the Cathedral — and of Rainaldo who continued on the same work) begun, in this turn, the grandiose Baptistry. Later Bonanno PISANO started the construction of the Leaning Tower and at a certain moment works ceased, to remain untouched for 90 years. Afterwards came GIOVANNI DI SIMONE, who built other stories on the same style as those of the originator of this grandiose architectural work and about the middle of the 15th century, TOMMASO, son of ANDREA PISANO, finished the tower with the construction of the belfry. This latter master also took an interest in the architecture of the Churchyard. In these masterpieces of art, constructed during the period of major economical prosperity because of the marine enterprises of the Republic of Pisa, there is a wonderful combination of

*On the left: **A foreshortening of Piazza dei Miracoli seen from the antique «Porta Nuova».** Below: **Piazza dei Miracoli. It is in this great simplicity of nature that the white marble so wonderfully worked by human genius is best displayed.***

Romanesque, Longobard, Mussulman and Gothic architecture to shape a new style, called «Pisa Style».

Not only the architecture but also the sculpture of Pisa was grandiose. The names of GUGLIELMO PISANO, of BONANNO, of NICOLA PISANO and then of GIOVANNI, son of NICOLA, are sufficient for indicating the high level of this grandiose art. The masterpieces of this group can be favourably compared to the works of the masters.

GALIELO GALILEI, FIBONACCI, ANTONIO PACINOTTI, ULISSE DINI were all citizens of Pisa. These names alone are sufficient to establish the proud and great tradition of the town, together with its famous and ancient university.

In the field of painting Pisa takes a place considerably inferior to that occupied in architecture and scultpure. However, even if names of the more prominent artist are lacking there is no reason to overlook the names of GIUNTA DI PISA, that of the brothers TEDICE and the brothers VANNI, of FRANCESCO TRAINI, GIOVANNI DI NICOLA, CECCO DI PIETRO, AURELIO LOMI, ORAZIO RIMINALDI, G.B. TEMPESTI, MELANI and others.

CATHEDRAL SQUARE

The monuments which transform a common name of square into the «Piazza dei Miracoli» are: the CATHEDRAL, the BAPTISTRY, the BELL or LEANING TOWER and the HISTORICAL CHURCHYARD. A combination of works or architecture and sculpture which rise stately and austere, but at the same time refined

and full of charm, placed around a wide tender green lawn. It is in this natural semplicity that the white marbles, so highly worked and rendered precious by human genius, have found a perfect setting. Is is exactly in this pleasant semplicity of the «LAWN» that the greatness of the works, seem almost a creation of nature itself, wonderfully blended, so much so that the tourist, even if passing hastily by can't help but feel a strong sense of admiration and in some cases emotion. This wonderfull architectural composition, with so much harmony of styles and colours, contrasts its beauty with that of the ancient walls facing west and east, as well as the buildings of the 14th century facing south, today seat of the «Spedali Riuniti di S. Chiara».

All this artistic magnificence on the whitness of the marbles, the pleasant green of the lawn, the various tonalities of the ancient walls with their embattlements, the sombre and solemn row of cypresses, form a whole really great, even touching play of lights at every hour of the day. In the evening the sight is perhaps even more beautiful because as the sun sets a dim and soft illumination substitutes its light, rendering the play of lights more suggestive and penetrating.

Portrait of Galileo Galilei by the Sustermans.

In the city's major monuments, the glorious traces of Pisa's Marine Republic are represented in basreliefs. The basrelief represented above, as with that below, contains the date of the beginning of the construction of the tower engraved on its base.

THE LEANING TOWER

This is the monument that, among the others of the «Piazza dei Miracoli» stirs the imagination of practically everybody, from the old to the young. Firstly we like to give you some information and events regarding its long history.

The construction of this imposing mass was started in the year 1174 by BONANNO PISANO. When the tower had reached its third storey operations ceased because it had started sinking into the ground. The tower remained thus for 90 years. It was completed after 99 years by GIOVANNI DI SIMONE, TOMMASO, son of ANDREA PISANO, crowned the tower with the belfry.

The top of the Leaning Tower can be reached by mounting the 294 steps which rise in the form of a spiral on the inner side of the tower walls.

The tower is 55.863 mts high.

Max height 56.705 mts.

The inside diameter at the base is 7.368 mts.

The outer diameter on the base is 15.484 mts.

There are 8 storeys.

It is supported by foundations of about 3 mts.

The Tower weights about 14,500 tons.

In the belfry there are 7 bells each one of them corresponding to a note of the musical scale.

Above: A view of the upper part of the tower, in a splendid framing which intersects an external detail of the right transept of the Cathedral. One can see how the architecture of the tower in its various elements forms a unitary relationship with the Cathedral (arches, small arches, capitals, small lodges, rhombi etc.). Below: Detail of a romanic capital at the base of the tower.

The oldest bell is that named «Pasquareccia» which rang to announce that the Earl Ugolino della Gherardesca, sentenced for treachery, was starving to death together with his sons and nephews in the tower of Piazza delle Sette Vie (today Piazza dei Cavalieri). On the top of the tower GALILEO GALILEI carried out famous experiments besides that regarding the affects of gravity. It is one of the seven wonders of the world. From the top we can enjoy a vast view, that starting from the Monte Pisano, the mountains of Garfagnana and the Apuanian Mountains slopes down towards us, demonstrating the great extent of the whole fertile plain, which, before reaching the sea, meets the grandiose and extensive forest regions of Migliarino and S. Rossore.

Art of the Tower

The very famous work is of Romanesque style, and as already stated dates back to the year 1174. Cylindrical in shape it demonstrates externally six open galleries. A cornice separates these galleries one from the other and each

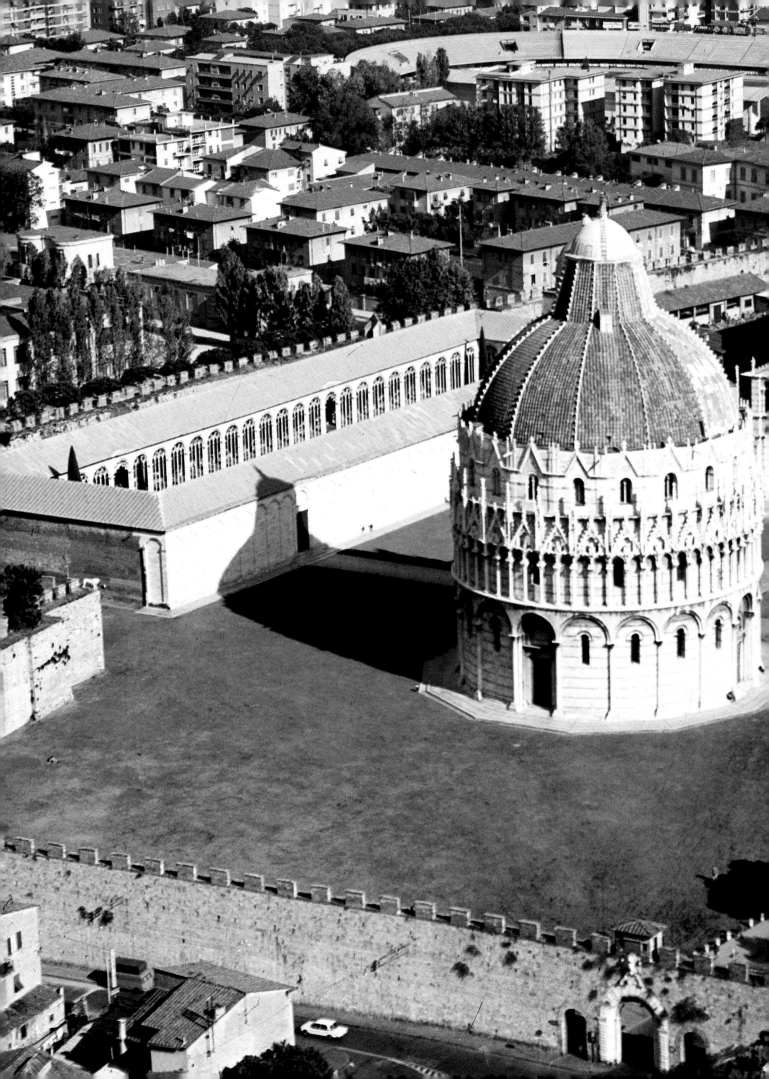

Above: A partial view of the sixth order of the small lodge and the bell tower decorated with arches resting on corbels or small columns which frame the opening. The tower was completed in 1350 by Andrea Pisano's son, Tommaso. On the left: The leaning tower flanked by the column carrying the Greek bowl, a copy of the original which is in the Monumental Cemetery (see page 65). On the right: A view of the tower and the right transept of the Cathedral.

presents a series of small arches fitted on the capitals of the slender columns. In the base there is a series of big blind arcades, between which elaborate and geometrical designes have been executed. In the belfry there is the same design or arcades as that of the base, with the difference that here, there are, apart from the reduced proportions, apertures or doors for the movement of the bells.

Although stately, this monument is not lacking in elegance and lightness due to this dense location of arcades and open galleries between one storey and another. The entrance is surmounted by a lunette on which is sculptured a work of Andrea Guardi, that is the «Madonna with Enfant, St. Peter and St. John».

Although it can be considered a real masterpiece of architecture, this monument is mostly famous for its strong inclination. Regarding this inclination it can be safely stated that is undoubtely due to a sinking of the ground right from the time of its construction. Therefore, for those who desire to imagine that great tower was intentionally built inclined, this assumption is entirely without foundation. Unfortunately, even today the great mass continues to sink very slowly. It is a question of about 1 mm. every year. Since nodoby can state with matematical security that this sinking effect will continue in the future at the present yearly rate, without its ceasing, remedies by means of adequate mesures, based on scientific studies and projects, are under consideration. In the meantime supervision of the effect with instruments of very high precision is continously being carried out.

THE CATHEDRAL

This grandiose masterpiece of Romanesque-Pisa Style was started in the year 1063 by the great architect BUSCHETTO. It is, therefore, the first work undertaken in the spot that became later the «Piazza dei Miracoli». It was possible because of the enormous wealth amassed by the powerful Sea Republic which at that time Pisa was, particularly after having carried out a fruitful excursion on Palermo. The Cathedral was consecrated in the year 1118, even though still incomplete, by Pope Gelasio the 2nd. It was terminated in the 13th century, with the erection of the façade, unchanged up to today, by RAINALDO, who also built the main apse.

The Cathedral, designed in Latin-Cruciform, basically has a romanesque architectural style, but at the same time

On the left: **The Cathedral's face.** *Above:* **The dome seen from the top of the tower.** *On the right:* **A detail of the Cathedral's face.**

interpretes and absorbes elements of the styles of various periods, forming thus a unique style which has something of sublime. The Cathedral was adorned, a little at the time trough the years, with numerous works of art. GIOVANNI PISANO is certainly the artist who excels in these works, specially because he has given us the famous, extremely rich and ingenious PERGAMO (Pulpit).

For a brief idea of its dimensions, the Cathedral is one hundred meters long. The façade is 35.40 mts wide. It is 34.20 mts high; hence both imposing and of an ingenious and grandiose conception.

The Facade of the Cathedral

The façade of the cathedral is articulated in five orders of arches, the inferior of which has seven blind arches, two laterals and one central gate, separated by columns and coupled pilasters. In the year 1595 a furious fire broke out and destroyed these gates (as well as the ceiling and other works on the inside) hence the gates of today, are not the original ones of the master BONANNO, but those made by the artists of the school of Giambologna, i.e. Francavilla, Mocchi, Tacca.

15

In the central gate is depicted the life of «Maria». The two laterals ones represent the life of the Redeemer. Still in this inferior order the walls are not lacking of numerous tarsia-rose-windows, groves, inlays of ornamental glass, geometrical panels to give a sense of grace and refinement.

The superior orders present open-galleries that contrast with the walls giving depth and movement so much so that the massive proportions of the whole façade becomes refined; and at the same time, rendered precious by a minute and elaborate fretwork.

Above the central gate, there is a memorial inscription of Rainaldo. The sarcophagus of BUSCHETTO, who started the construction of the cathedral, lays in the first arcade to the left. On the top of the façade, there is a statue of the Madonna of Andrea Pisano and at the sides angels of the School of Giovanni Pisano. At both sides of the first order of galleries there are the statues of two evangelists. The whole cathedral, both on the two sides and on the parts of the apses, repeats the decorative and ornamental themes of the façade, even if with slight differences. Also here, decorations are repeated as polychrome-tarsias, groved panels, inlays of coloured glass. The whole cathedral is a wonderful work of architecture and sculpture not at all lacking in grace in spite of its stately and massive conception.

The oval shaped dome is of a clear Gothic style: located at the intersection of the transept with the central body of the temple.

On the left: ***The central door of the Cathedral dominated by the mosaic of the lunette representing the Assumption of the Virgin and the bronze door whose panels tell of the Virgin's life.*** *On the right from top to bottom:* ***The panels recounting the Nativity and another episode from the Virgin's life.***
In the following pages: ***Scene of the Cathedral with a vertical aerial view of the Piazza dei Miracoli.***

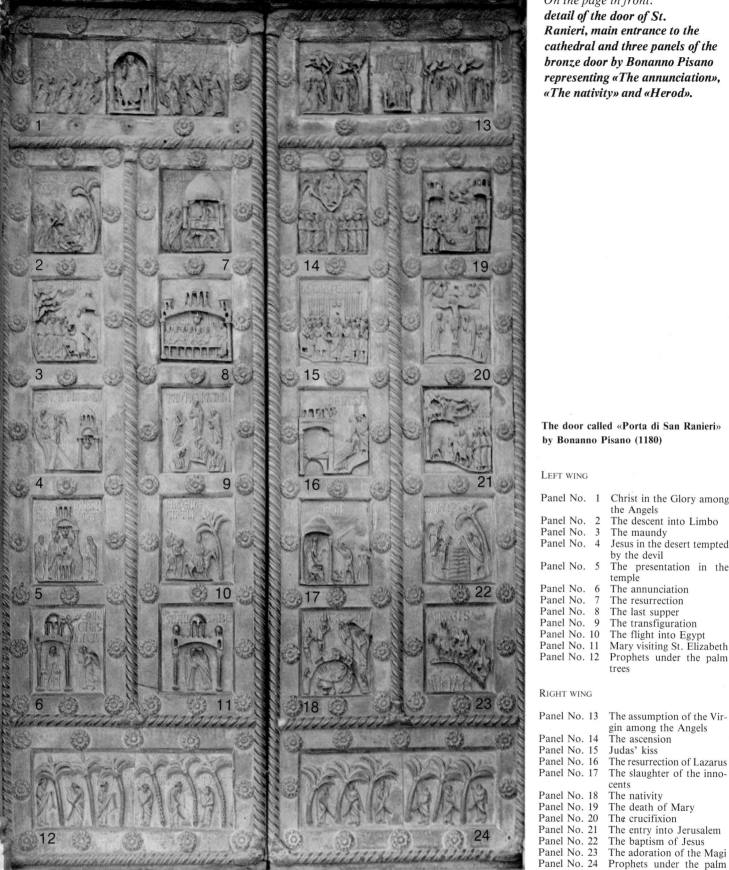

LEFT WING   RIGHT WING

On the page in front:
detail of the door of St. Ranieri, main entrance to the cathedral and three panels of the bronze door by Bonanno Pisano representing «The annunciation», «The nativity» and «Herod».

The door called «Porta di San Ranieri» by Bonanno Pisano (1180)

LEFT WING

Panel No.	1	Christ in the Glory among the Angels
Panel No.	2	The descent into Limbo
Panel No.	3	The maundy
Panel No.	4	Jesus in the desert tempted by the devil
Panel No.	5	The presentation in the temple
Panel No.	6	The annunciation
Panel No.	7	The resurrection
Panel No.	8	The last supper
Panel No.	9	The transfiguration
Panel No.	10	The flight into Egypt
Panel No.	11	Mary visiting St. Elizabeth
Panel No.	12	Prophets under the palm trees

RIGHT WING

Panel No.	13	The assumption of the Virgin among the Angels
Panel No.	14	The ascension
Panel No.	15	Judas' kiss
Panel No.	16	The resurrection of Lazarus
Panel No.	17	The slaughter of the innocents
Panel No.	18	The nativity
Panel No.	19	The death of Mary
Panel No.	20	The crucifixion
Panel No.	21	The entry into Jerusalem
Panel No.	22	The baptism of Jesus
Panel No.	23	The adoration of the Magi
Panel No.	24	Prophets under the palm trees

Normally, we enter into the cathedral from the gate of S. Ranieri (towerside). This gate, with its bronze pillars built by BONANNO PISANO is a masterpiece of art that shows traces of Hellenist c and Byzantine influences. It was built in the year 1180, and made up of 24 panels whereon are represented the «History of the Redeemer's life».

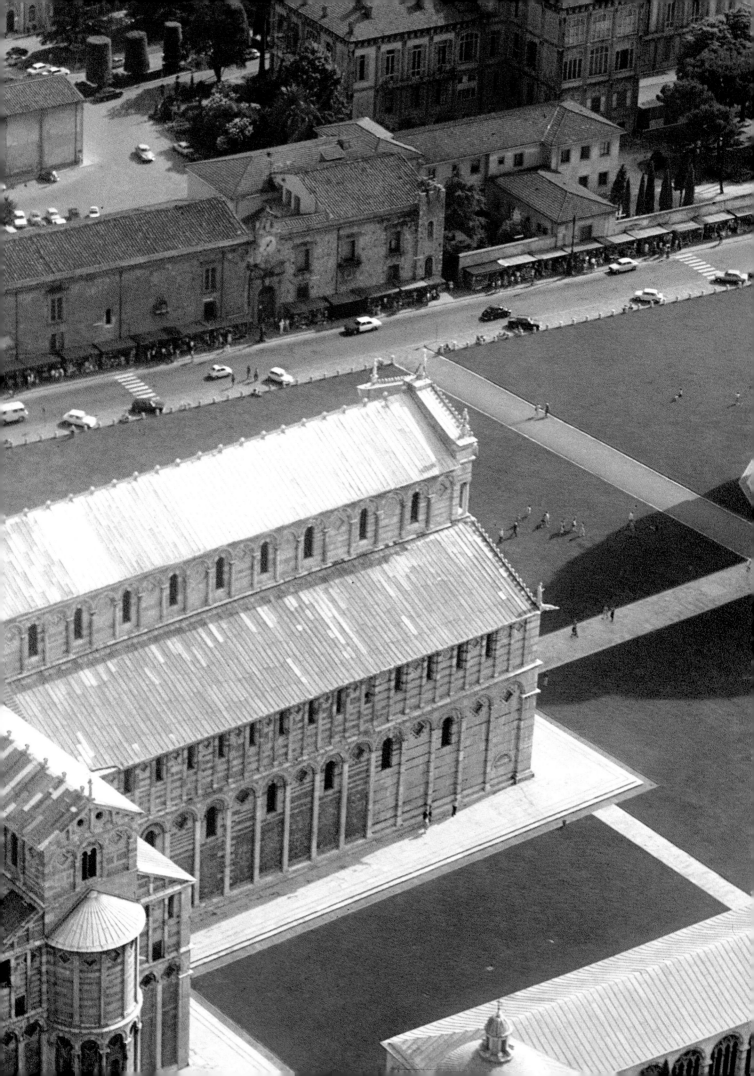

Interior of the Cathedral

In order to enjoy all the majesty of the temple, before stopping here and there, we advise you to go to the extremity with regards to the gate of St. Ranieri, from where usually entrance is allowed, i.e. to the inner wall of the cathedral façade. From here the view is total and its effect is such to convey a deep religion feeling. To this feeling is added a sense of bewilderment, as we stand before the vasteness and profundity of the spot and every architectural and sculptural work, as if not the hand of the man but a divine will had aimed at creating what we are admiring. If we place ourselves in the middle of the nave, at the inner wall of the cathedral, our attention will be drawn to the long, suggestive line of the imposing granite colonnades, which are almost all antique ande have capitals of Corinthian style. Then the women's gallery with little loggias located above the nave, the rich, highly decorated lacunar ceiling, the ample, profound, terminal apse whereon Christ on this throne contrasts, will complete our admiration.

In brief everything including the play of the minor colonnades, the black and white panels, which line the walls, shares to impart vivacity and movement to the grandiose realization of the temple.

Let us now pass to its description and to the visit. Internally it is divided into five aisles, one central major aisle and the minor ones two on each side. The transept has three aisles. Against the second line of columns of the central nave there are two holy water founts. The statues thereon are, on one side, Jesus and on the other side St. John the Baptist (17th century, of F. Palma).

Right Aisle - On the inner wall of the façade, looking towards the right aisles, there is the tomb of Matteo Rinuccini, over which hangs a bronze «Crucifix» of the 16th century, of P. Tacca. Moreover, frescoes painted in the 15th century by Pisan artists are to be noted on said wall. Along the long righthand wall there are four altars of STAGIO STAGI with paints of some, artists of the 17th and 18th century, such as CAVALLUCCI, TEMPESTI, CONCA, BEZZUOLI and others. Furthermore, there are inlaid seats of G. da Maiano and other artists.

At the 1st altar there is «The Virgin in her glory», of C. Allori, also named Bronzino.

At the 2nd altar «The dispute on the sacrament», of F. Vanni.

A the 3rd altar «The Madonna of the Graces», of Andrea del Sarto and G.A. Sogliani.

A the 4th altar there is, instead, a marble urn dominated by a lunette with a sculpture representing the «Almighty», valuable work of B. Ammannati.

Were are now at the right arm of the transept and turning towards we immediately see an altar with «Madonna sitting on a throne and Saints» made by Pierin del Vaga and G.A. Sogliani. High on the vault we can still see remanents of frescoes of P. del Vaga. Still further along the walls there are two large paintings of the 18th century. At the end of the arm in the centre there is the Chapel of St. Ranieri, work of architect B. Lorenzi. The sculptures are of the same author, see the statue of St. Efisio, as well as of F. Mosca, Stoldo Lorenzi, P. Guidotti. In the apse there is a

14th century mosaic, subjected to notable restauration, representing the «Madonna in her Glory»: it is a work of the 14th century.

On the opposite side of the transept, i.e. on the left hand wall facing the apse, we find the sarcophagus of the Emperor of Luxemburg Henry VII. This is very valuable work of Tino da Camaino. A part of this tomb is missing, and it is kept in a little room of the Churchyard «Camposanto Monumentale»: it depicts the figures of the Concillors. Immediately beyond the S. Ranieri Gate (normal entrance to the cathedral) there is an altar of Stagio Stagi and P. Fancelli with the central sculpture of «St. Biagio». Practically in front of this altar there is a holy water fount with a statue «Madonna with Infant», a work of Rossimino. Further down we reach the sacristy where the «treasures of the cathedral», consisting of relics, old illuminated codices, precious clothes and an ivory Madonna of Giovanni Pisano, are preserved.

The Presbytery - Is surrounded by a balustrade on which there are four angels; the two bronze ones are of GIAMBOLOGNA and his pupils; the other two in white marble, are of S. COSINI. Inside there are the remains of the ancient choral hall, that was almost completely destroyed together with the works by the famous paintings situated at the two pillars: the one on the right, facing the altar, is «St. Agnes» of Andrea del Sarto, to the left is the «Madonna with Infant» of G. Sogliani.

In the two chancels there are four extremely beautiful paintings of Andrea del Sarto: «St. Catherine» and «St. Margaret» to the right and to the left «St. Peter» and «St. John the Baptist».

On the High Altar - There is a bronze crucifix of GIAMBOLOGNA. Furthermore, there are six angels, a work of L. POLIAGHI. Following the APSE, where, at the entrance we find frescoes of M. CINGANELLI and an «ANGELS MUSICIANS» of GHIRLANDAIO. This later work has been repainted over the original version.

High in the Basin of the Apse - There is a large mosaic depicting «The Redeemer between the Blessed Virgin and St. John», this work was started by Francesco di Simone and finished by CIMABUE. Many other works letterally cover the whole apse behind the High Altar. There are paintings of Beccafumi with the «St. Matthew and St. Mark», others depicting scenes from the Bible and that of Moses breaking the Tables of the Law. Furthermore, there are works of Sogliani and Sodoma among which «The

*On the right: **An important view of the central nave. The image we see is striking: A long suggestive procession of majestic granite columns with Corinthian capitals, the women's gallery which is above the central nave and then the rich, extremely decorated lacunar ceiling. The image is completed by the wide and deep terminal apse where the «Christ on the Throne» shines out.***

Above: A special view of the Main Altar dominated by Giambologna's bronze crucifix of 1513, and in the lower order the six angels by L. Pogliaghi. On the page in front: The large mosaic of Jesus the All Powerful between the Virgin and San Giovanni which, begun by Francesco de Simone, was completed by Cimabue in 1302.

Deposition from the Cross», «The Sacrifice of Abraham», «St. Luke and S. John».

Other paintings are of R. Manetti, M. Rossell, P. Guidotti, A. Loni, O. Riminaldi.

Left Transept - On leaving the Presbytery we can immediately enter into the left transept where, along the right aisle, we find the «Tomb of the Archbishop of Elci», of G.B. Vacca, adorned with a tabernacle and a «Wooden Crucifix» of the School of Giovanni Pisano. Continuing along the ai-

sle there are paintings of P. Sorri, A. Lori, D. Passignano. Also to be noted is the 15th century white marble holy water fount of G. da Milano.

At the arm end, is the «Chapel of the Holy Sacrament», a work of B. Lorenzi. Here the sculptures are of F. Mosca (16th century). The altar and the bronze ciborium with silber parts are of the 17th century of G.B. Foggini. At the sides of the altar, in two niches, we see to the left «St. Mary Magdalene» and to the right «St. Christine» (C. Fancelli). In the basin of the apse there is a mosaic of the 14th century showing «The Annunciation». On continuing the visit and passing to the left wall of the trasept we se other paintings of the same authors of those on the right wall. At the end of this wall there is a marble altar of Stagio Stagi.

Left Aisle - Round the corner, after having visited the left arm of the transept, we enter directly into the main body of the Church, i.e. into the left aisle. Going towards the

façade, we find the first of the four altars of Stagio Stagi and in a lunette of this work we see the picture of «The Apparition of the Virgin to St. Ranieri» (B. Lorenzi). Continuing in the same direction are the following marble altars: «God in His Glory» of V. Salimbeni, the «Holy Ghost and Martyrs» of D. Passignano and «the Crucifix and the Saints» of G.B. Paggi.

At this point, very little remains to be done but to go to the center of the Cathedral to admire THE PULPIT, THE DOME, THE LAMP OF GALILEO.

The Cupola - Is above the right arm of the transept and is supported on imposing peak arches inspired by the Arabian-Muslam Style. It is ellipsoidal shaped. Both the pendentives and the vault have frescoes of Orazio and Girolamo Riminaldi with the «Assumption» on the vault, and with figures of Evangelists at the pendentives of Cinganelli.

Above, from the left: **The bronze chandelier realised from Battista Lorenzi's model in 1587. It is commonly called «Galileo's Lamp» because of a popular tradition according to which the famous Pisan Galileo Galieli had realised from the chandelier's oscillation the isochronism of the pendulum's oscillations. In reality we know that the scientist's discovery took place 6 years before the chandelier was deposited in the Cathedral, which took place in 1587.** *Above on the right:* **At the end of the transept's left arm is the Sacrament Chapel, a work by Battista Lorenzi. One can see the statues of Francesco Mosca which decorate the precious ciborium designed by Giovanni Battista Foggini.**

On the page in front: **Powerful and solemn, this frame is of the most significant part of the Cathedral's central nave. In the forefront is Giovanni Pisano's pulpit with its sculptured scenes, full of tension and animated by an almost dramatic emotivity; the Presbytery, the Main Altar dominated by the power of Giambologna's «Christ on the Cross» and finally the Apse which is rich in important paintings and dominated by the beauty of the mosaic «Jesus the Omnipotent», a work attributed to Cimabue, in the apse.**

OPERA DELLA PRIMAZIALE PISANA

CARTA D'INGRESSO ALLA CATTEDRALE

Esente da IVA - Art. 10 D.L. 26/10/72
n. 633 e successive modificazioni

VALIDO PER IL SOLO GIORNO DI EMISSIONE
VALID THE EMISSION DAY ONLY

VALID FOR ANOTHER MONUMENT:
SINOPIAS MUSEUM – DUOMO MUSEUM
MONUMENTAL CEMETERY
BAPTISTERY

VALIDO FUORI DELL'ORARIO DI CULTO
OUT OF CHURCH CEREMONY

CON DIRITTO DI ACCESSO AD UNO
DEI SEGUENTI MONUMENTI: MUSEO
DELLE SINOPIE - MUSEO DELL'OPERA
CAMPOSANTO MONUMENTALE
BATTISTERO

Per l'accesso ad altro Monumento o
Museo della Piazza del Duomo di Pisa

Cupon for admittance to another
Monument or Museum in the
Cathedral Square of Pisa

Der kontrollabschnitt für den Eintritt
in die anderen Gebäude und
Museen des Domplatzes in Pisa

Cupon de contrôle pour l'entrée
à un autre Monument ou Musée
dans laPlace du Dôme de Pisa

El cupón de control para el ingreso
a los otros Monumentos y Museos
de la Plaza del Duomo de Pisa

N⁰ ─ 94364

The Pulpit of the Cathedral

We are before a work of rare richness if not one of the greatest masterpieces. In this work the plasticity of the representation seems animated of sensibility and tension that's nearly dramatic.

Nicola Pisano, father of Giovanni, in his Pulpit in the Baptistry, for instance, expresses himself with a religious gravity that is possible to note in works of the Romanesque period. His son Giovanni in his work in the Cathedral, which we are now dealing with, has on the contrary completely renounced to this precise and calculated cold reproduction, giving breath and outlet to a vehement vivacity and to a deep human sense which comes to light from his figures.

The pulpit with its hexagonal base, work of Giovanni Pisano (1302-1311), is located near the first pillar of the vault. In the year 1599 it was dismantled and rebuilt only in the year 1926. It rests on eleven columnar supports that in turn rest respectively on lions others on pedestals. Other supports are represented by the statues of St. Michael, Hercules, the Evangelists supporting Chris and «The four Cardinal virtues» which, in turn, support the Church. The central represents «The Arts of the Trivium and Quadrivium». The capitals of the supports are sculptured with figures of Sibyl. In the lateral corbels there are Evangelists and Prophets. A cornice separates the above illustrated portion from the panels composing the upper portion of the pulpit and the figures of Prophets and Saints that are located between the panels.

In the panels are dramatically represented the events proceeding and following Christ's birth. They are:

1) Annunciation - Visitation - Birth of St. John the Baptist.

2) Birth of Jesus Christ.

3) The Wise Kings.

4) Presentation at the temple and the flight into Egypt.

5) The slaughter of the innocents.

6) The kiss of Judas - The arrest of Christ - The scourging of Christ.

7) The Crucifixion.

8) The chosen one.

9) The reprobates.

On the left: **The pulpit of the Cathedral, a genial work carved by Giovanni Pisano between 1302 and 1311.**

On the right:

The Caryatids - *In this celebrated marble group a mother breast feeds her two children. The artist, Giovanni Pisano, confronts a new religious theme. Clearly there is represented the allegorical image of the Church. The two babies hed in the arms of the woman represent the Old and New Testament. The four figures who support them at the base are the four cardinal virtues.*
The theological discourse of the sculpture in this artwork is of an exceptional clearness. It reaches a realistic expression of the Tuscany influence.

33

*Details of Giovanni Pisano's pulpit. On the left: **The naked Hercules with the club in his left hand.** Above: **The Nativity and the Flight to Egypt.** On the page in front: **The Crucifixion and the Slaughter of the Innocents.***

On the left:

Virgin with Child - *The Virgin with Child was completed by Antonio Sogliani (1492-1544). The artwork reflects the Tuscany style. In the performance of this artwork he chose the Raffaellean theme enhancing the gentleness and refinement typical of the great master, Raffaello Sanzio.*

On the right:

St. Agnes - *The artwork is of Andrea del Santo. It is one of the most famous artworks conserved at the Cathedral. In this piece of art are accentuated all the pictorial tendencies of the first Renaissance: design, color, atmosphere. The artist is a careful observer of the Leonardian style. He succeeds to carry into his paintings a personal sign of perfection from the technicalchromatic point of view.*

Here above:

The Urn of San Ranieri - *San Ranieri, patron saint of the city, is buried in the Great Sarcophagus located behind the altar of the chapel dedicated to him. He died in 1161. His body was preserved until 1591 in a more modest urn. This artwork was completed by G.B. Foggini in 1688. The rich marble was donated by Cosimo III, the Grand duke of Tuscany, and the Grand Duchess Vittoria of Rovere.*

On the left: **The monumental tomb of Henry VII, Emperor of Luxemburg, a work by Tino da Camaino.**

On the right: **The powerful work of the Baptistry. Begun in 1153 by the architect Diotisalvi, the project also saw the involvement of Nicola Pisano in 1260 and was completed in 1500 under the guide of Cellino di Neve and Zimbellino Bolognese.**

THE BAPTISTRY

It is located in front of the cathedral façade. The construction of this great building begun in the year 1153 under the guide of the architect DIOTISALVI, as stated on an epigraph situated inside the monument on a pillar. Hence it was the second monument to rise in the square, given that the works of the church belltower (or Leaning Tower) begun many years later, i.e. in the year 1174. Also in the case of the Baptistry its construction progressed as for the other monument of the «Piazza dei Miracoli», i.e. from the beginning to the end of the works many years lapsed due to interruptions of different causes. In fact, only in the year 1260, under the guide of Nicola Pisano, when the works were practically suspended, they restarted with a certain alacrity. Only at the end of the 14th century the work terminated unter the guide of CELLINO DI NEVE and ZIMBELLINO BOLOGNESE.

The Baptistry has a circular base, presents three orders (or stories) and from the third order (or Tambour) rises the dome. The height of this imposing monument is 55 mts, with a diameter of 35.50 mts. It has four gates, the principal of which opens towards the façade of the Cathedral.

In spite of its gigantic mass, its aspect is refined by a multiple series of ornaments in Gothic style.

The first storey is with blind arcades like the Leaning Tower and the Cathedral but with the variation that in this work windows have single apertures. The second order or storey presents an open gallery surmounted by ornamental aedicules with «busts». There are, furthermore, cusps, on which rest statues of Nicola PISANO and of his school. Such sculptures which, as we have said, are both in the niches and in the cusps of this second storey, are in the most part substituted by copies, while the originals are partly at the National Museum of St. Matteo and partly in the Baptistry itself. Other cusps magnificently rise, between the aedicules and minor cusps, extending beyond the second order or storey, up to the third order (or tambour), at the same height of the extremely beautiful mullioned windows which are the main ornament of this storey. Above the third order or storey rises the dome whereon there are other windows between the ribs. Regarding the «Entrance Gate» which is in front of the Cathedral façade we will simply list the art represented on this great portal. Here are the sculptures of an unknown author of the 13th century. On the right hand-post are depicted in relief «The Apostels», «The Descent into Hell» and «David». On the left hand-post are represented «The Months of the Year». The two fillet-architrave presents on the upper part «Jesus between the Virgin and the Baptist, Angels and Evangelists». On the inferior part there are «The History of the Baptist». Above the architrave opens a lunette, that in its centre depicts a copy of the Madonna of Giovanni Pisano. The original of this Madonna of the great master is in the Museum of the «Opera del Duomo». In the sculptured underarch of the lunette there are shown «The Agnus Dei» and «The 24 Seniors». Also the other portal that faces the walls of the «Churchyard» is magnificently decorated. In the architrave there is a sculpture with «The Annunciation and Saints».

Interior of the Baptistry

On entering the baptistry, the immensity of the building is even more convincing than from outside. Here, in fact, we obtain an immediate sense of the proportions. We have stated that the height is 55 mts and the diameter 35.50 mts: bare values, but from the inside, at this moment, the height and amplitude have another meaning, so penetrating as to cause admiration and dismay. We are, in fact, under the huge vault of the dome and in front of a grandiose annular nave lighted almost with discretion by the numerous windows distributed all around. We are facing an imposing and high colonnade alternated with pillars that detached from the wall, delimitate a nave. Above is a very wide gallery with high arcades well lighted by windows.

The Pulpit of the Baptistry

This is a great work of the year 1260 of NICOLA PISANO. The artist for realizing the last panel of this opera, availed himself of the work of his still very young son Giovanni and of ARNOLFO DI CAMBIO, both of which later, cooperated with Andrea Pisano in realizing the pulpit for the cathedral of Siena. The pulpit of the baptistry has a hexagonal base supported by seven columns, three of which rest on supporting lions, on the sides. The central column rests a base depcting sculptured animal and human figures. This work evidently reveals a marked inspiration of the artist to the romanesque art of this time and a need to

Above right: Revealing view of the interior and the Pulpit (1260) by Nino Pisano. Below: The Adoration of the Magi and Matthew the Evangelist with one of the small figures between one arch and the next which depict Charity, Fortitude, Humility, Faith, Innocence and Hope (Pulpit details).

41

On the left: **The Baptistry pulpit by the sculptor Nicola Pisano, carved between 1255 and 1260. In this work the artist reaches the apex of his creative and artistic capacity and it signifies a memorable moment for Italian sculpture. The pulpit has a hexagonal base, supported by 6 external columns, three of which rest on upright lions and a central column which is placed on a pedestal carved with animal and human figures. The three orders of figures which are represented are the indication of the artist's wide and** complex cultural learning. **At the base are the lions expressing the natural forces, while at the centre are the spiritual forces whose reign is expressed by Virtue and the Prophets. In the upper order are the events from the life of Christ which take us to the memory of history.**
Here above: A detail of the pulpit featuring the Adoration of the Magi.

Details of the pulpit. On the left: **The panel of the Nativity, an upright lion, and a trilobate arch with the figure of the Envangelist Matthew.** *Above:* **The Presentation at the Temple and the Universal Judgement.** *On the right:* **The very beautiful nude figure representing Humility.**

express himself with a composed piety. Nevertheless it is not lacking in poetry even though it doesn't seem to exhalt a human sense of inspiration, that which on the other hand his son Giovanni desired and later manifested in the grandiose realization of the pulpit of the cathedral.

In the pendentives of the little arches there are figures of «Prophets». In the pillars of the corners are depicted: «Faith», «Charity», «Force», «Humility», «Fedelity» and «Innocence». In the panels there are represented:

1) The Nativity and Announcement to the Shepherds.
2) The Adoration of the Wise Kings.
3) The Presentation at the Temple.
4) The Crucifixion.
5) The last Judgement.

In the baptistry if one asks the attendents, it is interesting to hear the echo. On the inside for instance, a melody reechoes many times through the ample vault and it gives the impression of hearing a strange, harmonious and multitoned big organ.

45

*Above: **The Font with the Altar and Pulpit.** On the left: **One of the various rosettes which decorate the font.***

Baptistry Fountain

Our attention will be very soon drawn by the Font and the Pulpit. The font is located in the middle of the temple on three steps. It is a work of the 13th century of G. DA COMO. The big octagonal basin, which incorporates other four smaller basins, was realized for baptism by immersion. In the middle of the basin there is a beautiful statue of the Baptist, a work of ITALO GRISELLI. The font is enriched with eight faces decorated by central rose-windows and by geometrical marble decorations. The altar, located close to the font is composed of six panels with marble inlays and rose-windows. It is surrounded by inlaid seats of the 17th century. Looking towards the altar we can appreciate cosmati-floor of the 14th century.

The Hebrew Cemetery and Synagogue

From the 18th century the Jewish community of Pisa began to inter their deceased in this very tranquil area full of peace and srenity. In earlier times the Hebrew cemetery was located in the quarter of Porta Nuova.

The power of the Marine Republic of Pisa was well known and influential in the far off eastern countries. Evidently, many citizens of Pisa during their travels and commercial activities came into contact with the Hebrew communities of these countries. There is information concerning the first information concerning the first Hebrews who lived in Pisa dating from 1165 onwards. The community was relatively emarginated with respect to the remainder of the local population. The lived in the area commonly called the «Chiasso dei Giudei» (Alley of the Jews).

Such a positive function has continued throughout the following centuries. This brought considerable prestige to the Israelite community of Pisa. The population reached to nearly one thousand persons. Only the racial laws succeeded to dismember it. Such resulted in a great loss to the city.

The Hebrew Cemetery.   *The Sinagogue Interior.*

The Etruscan Lion

Different and discordant are the opinions of the experts on the origins of the lion which is implanted on the Medici walls. There are those who hold that the artwork is absolutely Etruscan. And there are those who speak of Roman artwork with strong oriental influences.

It is certain that the power of this lion recalls a world which has passed; a world where economy and commerce were the basic motives of political life of the city and the state.

47

THE MONUMENTAL CEMETERY

Coming out of the baptistry and looking once more at the majestic façade of the cathedral on will see to the left the churchyard which presents its long marble walls in the form of a rectangle. These boundary walls are composed of blindarcades on pilasters similar to those of the cathedral, tower and baptistry just visited. In these walls there are two entrances in the arcades. The main gate is on the right to the cathedral, over which stands out a Gothic three-cusped tabernacle with «Madonna and Saints». It is a work of Giovanni Pisano and his school.

Before passing over to the description of other things, it is to be said that the churchyard is a work that dates back to about the end of the 13th century and was started by GIOVANNI DI SIMONE. Centuries passed before it was ultimated, just as for the other monuments of the square.

It is said that the archbishop Ubaldo de' Lanfranchi, in 1203, brought earth from the Golgotha Mountain with galleys coming back from a crusade, because it seems that this earth was capable of reducing a body into a skeleton within twenty four hours. When Giovanni di Simone started the works the churchyard already existed. In fact, the aim of this monumental work as started by him was to gather within a limited area in an orderly and dignified manner all the graves scattered around the cathedral and at the same

*On the left, above: **The enormous construction of the Monumental Cemetery which is almost too linear and unitary, is broken up by the attractive gothic decoration of the tabernacle.** Below: **The Tabernacle. The Virgin on the throne surrounded by four saints and a personage who is on his knees in the middle of his devotions while the whole is placed in the attractive interior of the tabernacle. The work was carried out in the second half of the fourteenth century presumably by a follower of Giovanni Pisano who reminds one of the unique grace of the great maestro.** Here above: A view of the interior of the Monumental Cemetery.*

time to leave space for others in the future as was the deep rooted tradition of the noble families of Pisa of this time.

Later, ancient sculptures, sepulchral monuments, works or art scattered around the city, were gathered inside the churchyard. Sarcofagi of famous men lined the walls, that were frescoed by different, great artists. All this rendered the «Camposanto Monumentale» (Monumental churchyard) of Pisa, progressively as time passed, one of the greatest and richest galleries of medieval painting and sculture, besides representing a great masterpiece of architecture. During the 2nd World War this enormous artistic and cultural patrimony suffered severe damage and losses. During the bombing raid of the 27th July 1944 a big fresco of Sienese-school was destroyed and the many frescoes of Gozzoli were badly damaged. The roof caught fire melting the lead-plates covering the roof and the molten lead dropped down on the works of art. Today many of there works have benn restored but have not been situated in their original places but temporaly scattered here and there around the walls. Others are located in appropriate rooms.

The Churchyard from Inside

On entering the churchyard ones attention is immediately drawn to the great colonnade that opens out on an inner lawn with its great, round arcades. These latter are each adorned by four apertured amall windows with fine, plurilobed, little arches.

Furthermore, looking around at the walls of the colonnade and seeing only the remains of frescoes we cann't but feel a deep sorrow in thinking what our eyes could have admired today if the range of the 2nd World War had saved this monumental spot with everything in its place. Saddened by this thought now it remains to content oneself by immagining the precious art gallery as it was before the war and looking for the works remaining removed to be restored. For some of these pieces, special rooms have been arranged: see that for the «Triumph of the Death», «The Last Judgement», «The Anchorets» and the other for the Ruddle-works of GOZZOLI and for the very important Romanesque and Gothic sculptures and bas-riliefs. Concerning the ruddle-works, which are the preparatory sketches of the frescoes, brought to light when the same frescoes were detached from the wall for restauration, it is to be said that they are of great interest.

Another scene of the interior of the Monumental Cemetery.

QVAMVIS PECCATRIX SVM DOMNA VOCATA BEATRIX
IN TVMVLO MISSA IACEO QVAE COMITISSA
A D M LXXVI

On the left, above: **Wall with frescoes and Greek and Roman sarcophagi.** Below: **A famous Greek-Roman sarcophagus from the Second Century containing the story of Hippolytus and Fedra. The carved images in bas-relief represent an episode of mythological nature as was the custom at the time. Nicola Pisano was, for a long period of time, inspired by these before carrying out his famous pulpit in the Baptistry. It was used in 1076 as a tomb for Countess Beatrice of Canossa, mother of Mathilde of Tuscany.** Above: **A Greek sarcophagus with hunting scenes.**

On the right:
During the glorius times of the powerful Marine Republic, these chains served to close the gates of the city of Pisa. For the citizens of Pisa they represent the sad memory of the Battle of Meloria during which the city was badly beaten by the rival Republic of Genoa.
The chains were immediately restituted to Pisa after the independence of Itali. On the stone commemoration tablet is read, «to the perennial and fraternal affection, harmony and union hereafter indissoluble».

The Triumph of Death: the scene represents a riding party who are going hunting. The group consists of powerful nobles, ladies of the court and knights with their trail of helpers, arm-carriers, game and dogs. The party stops in front of three open coffins containing the remains of the King. Alongside is Macarius, an anchorite saint who is intent on teaching the party how life is vain when confronted with the reality, although disturbing but true, of the Triumph of Death. For her, we are all equal: power, vanity, wealth have no meaning and nor does the social level to which one belons.

And it is in fact prevalently towards the powerful, the upper classes that it refers, showing that they, like everyone else, cannot escape their inexorable destiny.

The details of the page opposite effectively show the significant behaviour and expressions of the various characters in the scene giving them great movement and a strong meaning to the work's theme.

54

The Last Judgement

Above, we see the celestial hierarchy with Christ and Our Lady inside two «mandorlas», in the middle, and the twelve apostles on both sides. Below, trumpeting angels calling together the bodies who have come out from the tombs, and, further down in the middle, the Archangel Michael with drawn sword, dividing the chosen souls (on the left) from the reprobates. Finally, at the bottom there are the two hosts of the blessed and of the damned.

Hell

The fresco is dominated by the terrible, huge figure of Lucifer around which a rocky hell is depicted: in the circles, the naked and tortured bodies of the damned mix with the monster-like bodies of their persecutors, the devils.

58

The frescoes which recount the story of San Ranieri were once found on the wall of the southern wing of the cemetery; now restored they can be found in a room which has been deliberately set up in the same wing. These frescoes are almost totally the work of the florentine Andrea Bonaiuto who painted them around 1377 and Antonio Veneziano who worked on them between 1384 and 1388. In the details on this page one can see some episodes from San Ranieri's life: his trip to the Holy Land, his return to Pisa and his pastoral permanence in the city.

Spinello Aretino: S.` Efisio fights against the infidels. ➞

60

THE MUSEUM OF THE CATHEDRAL VESTRY BOARD

The museum contains works which used to adorn the monuments of the Piazza dei Miracoli and which, mainly for safety reasons, had been moved to the warehouses of the Cathedral Vestry Board. It was set up in 1986 in a specially restored building, between Piazza dell'Arcivescovado and Piazza del Duomo, which had been originally designed as a capitular seat (13th century) and then turned into an enclosure monastery. The exhibition takes up rooms on two different floors and the visit is made pleasant by the variety of works displayed and by an exceptionally good set of captions.

On the ground floor the following works are of particular value: the wooden crucifix by Borgognone; the bronze hippo-gryph; the Citharoedus David; the Madonnas by Giovanni Pisano, particularly the so-called «Madonna del Colloquio» and the ivory small statue; the sculptures by Tino di Camaino, by Nino and Tommaso Pisano, by Andrea Guardi, etc.; the precious objects forming the «Treasure», with the crucifix by Giovanni Pisano, the Limoges caskets and the «Cathedral's belt»; the silverware of the Cathedral sacristy. On the upper floor: large paintings on canvas; some of the Cathedral's old fittings together with some precious wooden marquetries; miniated parchments; sacred vestments; printings of the 19th century representing the frescoes of the Camposanto and a rich archeological collection with Roman, Etruscan and Egyptian objects.

These works flow before visitors along the museum path, thus reminding them of the events which accompanied the life of the monuments and of the town of Pisa: the Islamic influences, the sculptures of the 14th century, the spiritual inheritance of the ancient Rome.

1) Entrance to the Museum. 2) Busts lined up in the interior of the cloister portico. 3) Our Lady with Child, an ivory work by G. Pisano. 4) Julius Caesar's head. 5) «Alcove» hall. 6) Hall with a sculpture by G. Pisano. 7) Our Lady with Child known as the «Madonna of the Talk». 8) John the Baptist, by G. Pisano.

3

5

4

6

7

8

THE MUSEUM OF THE SINOPIES

The museum has been set up in a time-battered hospital pavilion, restored in 1979, which was part of a building erected in 1257 by Giovanni di Simone, the same architect who, later on, would build the Monumental Cemetery. The historical link between these two constructions was to manifest itself again after centuries. In 1944 the Cemetery was devastated by a fire during which the works of art preserved in its rooms and, above all, the famous fresco cycle painted on its walls, were badly damaged. The following peeling off of the damaged frescoes, which was a necessary stage of the restoration, has brought to light the preparatory sketches which had been hidden by the plaster. The

discovery of the sinopies, whose name comes from the Turkish town of Sinope which supplied the earth used as colouring matter to paint them, has been a major artistic event, both because these works had remained unseen up to that time and because, thanks to the freshness of their execution, they sometimes are more valuable than the corresponding frescoes. The fifty or so sketches displayed in the museum were painted on the walls of the Camposanto in the 14th and 15th century and represent undoubtedly the biggest collection of its kind. The artists are those considered as the authors of the Camposanto frescoes: Buonamico di Buffalmacco, Francesco Traini, Antonio Veneziano, Spinello Aretino, Taddeo Gaddi, Piero di Puccio and Benozzo Gozzoli.

On the upper floors visitors walk on modern modular structures; photographic reproductions on panels of the most important frescoes allow comparisons which reveal the author's insights and changes of mind during the tormenting phases of the thinking up and execution of the paintings.

Finally, it is advisable to visit the Monumental Cemetery in order to complete the information acquired in the Museum of the Sinopies.

Museum opening times:
9 to 12.30 a.m. - 3 to 7 p.m. during the summer; 9 to 12.30 a.m. - 3 to 4.30 p.m. during the winter. The change from the summer to the winter opening times occurs gradually, following the length of daylight.

1. Museum; 2. Stories of Agar and Abraham: Abraham; 3-4. Sinopy and fresco of a detail of the Last Judgement; 5. The Archangel Michael; 6. The wedding of Isaac and Rebecca: Abraham and Eliezer; 7. The worshipping Magi: a Magi King; 8. Stories of the anchorities: left lower part.

64

5

6

7

8

HORSEMEN'S SQUARE

After the «Piazza dei Miracoli» we would suggest to start the visit of the town from the «Piazza dei Cavalieri», not only becauseeit is the most important and beautiful square, after that of the cathedral, but also because it is nearby. Leaving the cathedral and entering the old Via S. Maria and after along Via dei Mille, we come out at Piazza dei Cavalieri. We find here a group of buildings that surrounded it irregularly but at the same time with an extraordinary harmony. We notice at once the Palace of the Knight's Caravan (after wich the square is named), and where now seats the Superior Normal College. Beyond that, we see the National Church of St. Stephen of the Knights. The Clock Palace is on the left of the entrance of the Via dei Mille. On the opposite side of the Clock Palace, there is the Palace of Puteano College and the Council Palace of the Order of St. Stephen. The fountain located in the square is a work of the year 1596 of P. Francavilla. In proximity to it is the statue of Cosimo the 1st de' Medici, who founded the Order of the Knights of St. Stephen.

NATIONAL CHURCH OF ST. STEPHEN OF THE KNIGHTS

This is an opera of the 16th century of Vasari who, later, built also the bell-tower in 1572. The church presents a marble façade of Don Giovanni de' Medici (1606) with a single portal in the middle, above which is the Emblem of the Knights Order. Flanking the sides of the church are two wings that were once used as dressing-rooms for the knights of the order of St. Stephen. These are later transformed into two aisles of the cqrch by Pier Francesco Silvani.

The inside - Is a nave with an extremely beautiful wooden inlaid celling. In each of the six partitions, into which it is divided, is a painting represent «The glory of the knights». These works are of C. Allori, Empoli, Ligozzi and Cigoli.

On entering the church we can admire two precious holy

water founts of Vasari while, on the right and left hand wall, we see in high between the windows, four ship lanterns. These same walls are hung with tapestry and flags captured from the Turks. In this church there are also figureheads of ships of St. Stephens Order. Still on the wall we see four distempers (two on each side) representing «Episodes of St. Stephen Life», work of Vasari, Empoli, Allori and Ligozzi. To be noted also is the small but precious marble pulpit of the year 1627 of C. Fancelli. The walls of the church have four doors — two on both sides — which open into the two aisles that, as previously mentioned, were used as dressingrooms for the Knights of St. Stephen.

In the right aisle at the first altar we see the «Lapidation of St. Stephen» of G. Vasari. At the second altar there is a crucifix of Tacca. In the left aisle at the first altar, near the exit of the church, there is «The miracle of the loaves and fishes» of Buti; at the second altar the «Nativity of Jesus» opera of Bronzino.

The monument to Cosimo I de' Medici by Francavilla.

At the high altar there is the sarcophag of St. Stephen Pope (P.F. Silvani and Giovan Battista Foggini, 1700). Behind the altar a gilt bronze bust of «St. Lussorio» of Donatello is preserved under a glass-bell.

Of the palaces which surround the square let us dwell a little upon that, that today is the seat of the Normal Superior School; a renovation of Vasari — 16th century — of the old Palace of the Elders of the Pisan Republic. This building was appointed by Cosimo the 1th de' Medici to receive the military order of knight of St. Stephen, hence it was also called «Palace of the Caravan». Observe the originality of the building, its slight curvature with a graffito-decorated façade, with a series of busts of the Grand Dukes of Tuscany of that time at the second storey and in the middle, above a balcony, the escutcheon of the Medici family.

Now we are in front of the original Palace of the Clock that is a successful architectural utilization of two ancient towers constructed from designs of Vasari, that is the tower of Gualandi (or Gherardesca) with the other of the TOWN-JAIL or Torre delle Sette Vie. In the tower of Gualandi inprisoned for treachery together with sons and nephews Count Ugolino starved to death. Count Ugolino was at that time Podestà of the town and the Marine Republic of Pisa had just suffered a clamorous defeat on the sea by the Republic of Genoa in the very famous battle of Meloria (1284).

Of minor turistic interest are the Palace Puteano of the 17th century and the Palace of the Council of the Order (Francavilla 1603), then seat of the Law-Court of St. Stephens' Order and today seat of the Superior School for applied sciences «A. Pacinotti».

The square of the Horsemen: On the left, the Gherardesca Palace with the Muda Tower: on the right, the Palace of the Horsemen.

Church of Santa Maria della Spina - *This jewel of Gothic art of Pisan-style is located on the Lungarno Gambacorti. Initially it was an oratory at the extreme limit of the Arno River. After is was enlarged by Lupo Capomaestro in 1323 and named Chiesa della Spina (church of the thorn) because it preserved one of the thorns of the Christ crown. In the year 1871, after about five hundred years, the church was dismantled piece by piece and rebuilt in a safer location away from the river waters that had badly damaged it. This very beautiful small church is covered with an extremly rich marble decorations of gentle contrasting colours and a suggestive series of cuspus and pinnacles.*

On the left: **The right side of St. Mary's Church of the Thorn with statues by Nino and Giovanni Pisano.**
Below: *Along the Arno.* Above: **The Basilica of St. Catherine built by the Domenicans in the second half of the thirteenth century.** On the right: **A marvellous altar-piece of the «Triumph of St. Thomas of Aquino», a work by Francesco Traini, situated in the abovementioned church.**
Below: **The church of St. Paul at Ripa d'Arno, built in the nineteenth century with a gothic-style front.** On the right: **The church's central nave.**

On the left:

Chapel of St. Agatha - *Is near the church of S. Paolo a Ripa D'Arno. It is Roman work, may be of DIOTISALVI, the great architect who built the Baptistry. It has an octagonal base with a piramid shaped dome. Observe the three-mullioned windows on the faces of the octagon.*

St. Frediano - *Is in the homonimous square and is of the 11th century. The church was founded by the family Buzzacherini Sismondi. The façade is Romanesque of Pisa-Lucca Style.*

St. Sistus - *Is of the year 1073 with façade of Verrucano and tuff pataere-decorations and majolica bowls of the 12th century. Inside there are three naves, the major of which incorporates itself semicircularly with the ancient church of S. Rocco.*

Above:

Abbey of St. Zeno - *Already existing in the 10th century, there is annexed to it the Camaldolite Monastery. It has been restored many times. Most recently, restoration has been undertaken after the damages suffered through the last war. The restorations have faithfully integrated the several architectonic lines typical of different periods.*

Right:

Church of the Holy Sepulcre - *This Romanesque church, with an octagonal base, built in 1153 by the architect DIOTISALVI, is located in the homonimous square by the Lungarno.*

73

NATIONAL MUSEUM OF ST. MATTHEW

The National Museum of Pisa can be rightly considered one of the most important in Europe especially for its collection of «PRIMITIVES». About the sculptures either in wood. stone or marble many of them are certainly unique. Here are present, in their completeness, the great masters of the fluorishing Pisa sculpture of the 12th and 13th centuries: NICOLA PISANO, BONANNO, GIOVANNI, ANDREA e NINO PISANO.

Also present are numerous works of TINO DA CAMAINO of Siena, without mentioning the many famous artists.

If at the beginning the aim of this gallery was to collect the works of the local art of said flourishing period, it is to be considered that this aim was largely surpassed, because neither their seat can be considered definitive (after the various movement of the works collected piece by piece through the centuries), nor can the room be considered sufficient because the continuous affluence of works, while

others are removed for reestablishing in their original places. The Museum has today its seat in an architectural complex that was initially a Benedictine nummery, then respectively town-jail and military barraks. As a consequence of all this, it was progressively transformed into its original structure and in 1945 new restoration works was started for receiving the works of art in the year 1949.

Above: «The Annunciating Angel», a sculpture in polychrome wood. On the left: The Cloister of the Museum of S. Matthew.

On top above: **The hall of wooden figures,
amongst which one can admire the «Announced
Virgin», a sculpture in polychrome wood by
Andrea Pisano.**
Alongside: **A Crucifix by Giunta Pisano, a work
carried out in tempera on board representing
Christ who is suffering humbly.** On the right:
Another admirable work by the same author.
Above: **maestro delle storie of San Galgano - San
Galgano**

Above:

St. Paul - *This magnificent panel was part of a polyptych completed by Masaccio in 1426 for the Church of Carmine at Pisa. The other five panels are scattered throughout several European museums. However, this panel is one of the most representative of the art of Masaccio Although he died early in life, he was one of the first to liberate himself from ties to gothic decadence, hence, laying the foundation for humanistic painting.*

On the left:

The Annunciation of the Virgin - *The Annunciation of the Virgin, delicate sculpture in polychromatic wood by Andrea Pisano.*

On the right: Madonna by Gentile da Fabriano.

SANCTVS·SEBASTIANVS·   ·SANCTVS·ROCHVS·

On the left: **San Sebastian and San Rocco by Domenico Ghirlandaio.** Above: **A magnificent polyptych of the Madonna with Child and Saints made by Simone Martini in 1320 for the church of St. Catherine.**
Right: **Taddeo di Bartolo - The crucifixion**

Below: altar-frontal by Francesco Traini - St. Dominic and two stories.

On the top-left: «The Madonna on the Throne with Child and Stories», a work by an unknown artist referred to as the «Maestro of San Martino». It is considered as the best work of the thirteenth century Pisan painting. On the same page: Details of the painting.

On the right:

The Madonna of Milk - *This masterpiece was completed by Nino Pisano during the first half of the 14th century under the auspices of the Church of the Thorn. It is a rare example of delicate refinement which distinguished the sculpture of Pisa during the epoch.*
The gentleness of the expression on the face of the Virgin as she watches with love. The Little Child who nourishes himself from her milk. This is typical of the humanity which may be noted in each artwork of this great artist from Pisa.

82

Above: **University of Pisa: The cloister and detail of the cloister;** *on the left:* **University of Pisa: Great Lecture Hall and the Botanical garden.**

THE UNIVERSITY

Situated in Via XXIX Maggio in a building of the 15th century of a scarce architectural value, the façade of which has been recently rebuilt.

The institution of the «Sapienza» goes back to very remote times; it is sufficient to say that it was founded in the 12th century and is, therefore, one of the most glorious and ancient among the Italian universities. Today in this university all the faculties are represented. It has a very rich library comprising interesting collections of scientific character and original documents, among which some written by Galileo Galilei himself. To be University is annexed also a Museum of Natural History and the Botanical Gardens.

84

Illumination of St. Ranieri - Takes place every year on the evening of the 16th June along the Lungarni. For this occasion also the Leaning Tower is illuminated. It is a phantasmagoric candlelight-illumination of the beautiful medieval palaces along the Lungarni, that so lighted reproduce fantastic reflections in the waters of the river, where at the same time hundreds of flickering lights slowly float down towards the sea. This sight, which draws thousands of the town-inhabitants and tourists, is crowned by an interesting fireworks display. This spectacle is in honour of the patron Saint of the town, whose feastday recurs the day after, on the 17th of June.

PALACES AND SQUARE

Even if antique squares, monuments, palaces, gates and towers worth visiting are numerous and scattered everywere over this town, of the more than ancient and glorious artistic and cultural traditions, we will limit ourselves to a general turistic glance. Up till now we have considered things of major renown and cultural interest just for a very short visit. We can now add, stil briefly, something about the marvellous «Lungarni», and about what may help the tourist for his knowledge regarding some historical and artistic elements he maylike to visit in a brief time.

The Agostini Palace - Another beautiful palace along the Lungarno is the Agostini Palace of the beginning of the 15th century, decorated by ornamental work of terracotta. This building is all the more interesting as it is the only one remaining in Pisa that demonstrated the architecture of buildings of Pisa decorated with reliefs. Here is also the CAFFÈ DELL'USSERO now renovated: it was the meeting-place of many patriots of the Risorgimento and of poets and writers.

Palace of the Giornata - This is a remarkable example of civil and Renaissance architecture. Once it was the property of the Lanfreducci family. Now it is the seat of the university rectorship.

The Gambacorti Palace - Starting from Piazza Garibaldi, across the Ponte di Mezzo, towards the right is the Gambacorti Palace of the 14th century, now seat of some municipal administrative offices. This building is of Gothic-Pisa style, three stories high with a beautiful maſade, mullioned windows, marble Corinthian columns and with three-lobe small arcades. It was built by Pietro Gambacorti who ruled the town. In the inside there is a hall called of the «Baleari» with frescoes of Melani, Fardella, Salimbeni (16th and 17th centuries).

The Toscanelli Palace - The version according to which this construction was built from a plan of Michelangiolo is not supported by the architectural conception which is evidently of an inferior level to that great master: today it is the seat of the State Records Office where ancient documents of Pisan history are filed. In this palace dwelt the great poet Byron in the year 1821.

The Medici Palace - Now seat of the Prefecture, is located in Piazza Mazzini, this one also faces the Arno River. It was built in the 13th century and remade in the 14th century appertaining at first to the D'Appiano Family then the

The Agostini palace

The Gambacorti palace

Palace of the Giornata

The Toscanelli palace

The Medici palace

The Campano tower

The Berlina square

The fortress and bridge on the Arno

Medici from the 15th century. It was also the dwelling of Lorenzo il Magnifico. On the beautiful façade there are two and three mullioned windows.

The Campano Tower - The «Campano» (big bell) which is located near the Market of Provisions, is so-called because the bell is of a very large dimension. The objective of the mammoth size was to project the sound to far away localities. In this way students were reminded that school lessons were about to begin.

The Berlina Square - In the medieval center of Pisa there is located the Plaza Cairoli, once called the Berlina. At one time in this plaza were exhibited the condemned to the «berlina» (pillory). Hence the derivation of the name of the plaza.

Old Stronghold (La Cittadella Vecchia) - Facing the Lungarno that runs alongside the church of St. Paolo a Ripa d'Arno and the homonimous place, we can admire the ancient Pisa-Fortress that is reflected in river waters. A wonderful sunset can be admired on this background when the sky is scattered with clouds tinted of different hues by the setting sun. This fortress of the old city was rebuilt and enlarged by Florentines who conquered Pisa in the 15th century. In 1558, Ferdinando I de' Medici built a ship-yard for the construction of galleys of St. Stephen Order. It was heavily damaged in 1944 by the rage of the war.

The Vendors' Loggias - The vendors' loggias were so named because originally they were used for the wool and silk market. They were erected in 1603 by order of the Grand duke Ferdinand I under the direction of the architect Cosimo Pugliani, from a design by Buontalenti of Florence. They are located nearby the Municipal Building.

The vendors Loggias

Old Pisan street in Borgo Stretto

89

The Monastery of Pisa - It rises in a fertile country among the valleys with their olive-trees and vineyards where peace and silence absolute reign. It was founded in the year 1366 and comprises church, cloisters, cells of the Carthusians and guest-rooms. Many are the works of a certain artistic importance and interest but the visitor will be mostly impressed by the charm due to the latebaroque style of the white buildings rich in marbles contrasting with the green of the surrounding countryside to create an atmosphere of elegance and at the same time a sensation of religiousness most appropriate to the setting. The tourist, after his visit to the Carthusian Monastery of Pisa, should not omit a visit to the Parish Church of Calci, romanesque art, founded at the end of the 11th century with its urn inside the high-altar containing the relics of Saint Ermolao, Patron Saint of the valley. The remains were placed in this church in the year 1111 by the Archbishop of Pisa Pietro Moriconi.

St. Peter at Grado - The origin of this ancient basilica is tied to a legend. In the 1880 Da Morrona wrote: «St. Peter on arriving from Antioch and when landing along the Tuscan shore, in a place called Grado, so named because of the steps, washed by the waves, where the boats landed, judged it an appropriate places for rising the first altar and temporarily founding a church». During recent escavations in fact, an ancient church of the 6th century was discovered located under the present one which was constructed in the 12th century.

The work is of Romanesque style, presents four apses and is made of tuff.

San Giuliano Terme: thermal bath.

THE HISTORICAL REGATTA AND FOLKLORE

Regatta of the Ancient Marine Republics - This takes place each year in June, alternately in one of the four ancient Marine Republics: Pisa, Genoa, Amalfi and Venice.

It is a competition in the Arno River (when the regatta takes place at Pisa), between the four opposing crews all in costume and on boats of that period. Before this regatta by night on the river it is certainly more interesting and spectacular to see the magnificent procession executed in costumes made from models of that period. In this procession are represented Kinzica de' Sismondi (a heroine of Pisa who saved the town from a fire caused by the Saracens) riding a white horse; the Duke of Amalfi, Guglielmo Embriaco of Genoa called Testa di Maglio, the Doge of Venice and Caterina Cornaro. Around all these personages there are armigers and captains, pageboys and damsels.

Game on the Bridge - Is a historic commemoration in costume on the Lungarno. Its origin goes back to the Roman Empire and perhaps even earlier. It takes place the first Sunday of June between opposite factions: North and South bank according to the natural division of the town by the river Arno. Formely this game was called «Gioco del Mazzascudo» (Game of club and shield) and was formally

Here above there is a wonderful image of women in costume and the people celebrating. In the background, there is the powerful image of the Cathedral.

disputed in Piazza dei Cavalieri (Knight's Square) — in that time named «Piazza degli Anziani» (Elders's Square) — of the Marine Republic of Pisa. Since 1490, following an ordinance of Lorenzo il Magnifico, the «Gioco del Mazzascudo» changed its name in «Gioco del Ponte» (Game on the Bridge) and takes place on the Ponte di Mezzo (Central Bridge).

Historical Regatta of St. Ranieri - Occurs the 17th June, feast of the Patron Saint of the town, in the Arno River with crews in costume manning antique style boats. People representing some quarters of the town take part in this game.

Parade in costume for the Historical Regatta

Historical regatta on the Arno

INDEX

An ivory Madonna with child by Giovanni Pisano, now situated in the Cathedral Museum.

Printed at the
Fotometalgrafica Emiliana printing press.
S. Lazzaro di Savena (Bologna)